POETRY OF ALMOST

A JOURNEY FROM HEARTBREAK TO HOPE

ABHISHEK SINGH

Made with ♥ on the Notion Press Platform
www.notionpress.com

Contents

Dedication

To the hearts that dared to feel too much,
To the souls who stayed soft after breaking,
To the ones who held on, and the ones who finally let go.

This book is for you.

For every silent cry, every almost love,
Every page you never got to write with them.
May you find yourself in the lines you now read.
And may these words remind you: You were always the story worth telling.

Foreword

I never meant to write a book just to make sense of the ache.

These poems began in silence, in sleepless nights and unsent messages. I wrote to survive, to remember, to let go. Somewhere between heartbreak and healing, the words found a rhythm, and I found a voice.

The "Poetry of Almost" is a story of love that almost was, and the self I found in its absence. It's for anyone who's ever held on too long, let go too late, or learned to love themselves in the ruins.

If something here feels like your story; it's because it is.

— Abhishek Singh

Preface

(A Poem Before the Poems)

This book began in a quiet room,

Where memories spoke louder than words.

It wasn't born from inspiration

It was born from ache,

From all the things I never got to say,

From all the times I broke in silence

And stitched myself back

With borrowed hope.

These aren't just poems

They're the echoes of someone learning

That healing doesn't come all at once.

It arrives in whispers, In shaky hands that still write

Even when the heart isn't sure

It knows how to hold a pen.

If you've ever loved too much,

Lost too quietly, Or stood at the edge of almost

Then maybe, These pages are yours too.

— Abhishek Singh

1. The Collapse

I spoke to the silence today,
And it whispered back your name.
The walls still hold our laughter,
But it doesn't sound the same.
The echoes of love still linger,
Like a ghost I cannot chase.
Everywhere I go, I see you
And nowhere do I find your face.

You left, but the silence you left behind still speaks your name.

You left, but your absence stayed,
Filling the spaces between my ribs.
I exhale, but it still hurts
Like a wound that never mends.
Your voice still hums in my ears,
Soft as the lies I believed.
You left without a goodbye,
Yet I'm the one who feels lost

Some goodbyes are never spoken, yet they echo the loudest.

• 5 •

I still set a place for you at the table,
Still leave space on my pillow.
My hands still reach for yours at night,
Only to find the weight of empty sheets.
Funny how we keep loving,
Even when love has left.
You're gone, but my heart still waits
For footsteps that will never return.

• 6 •

Love doesn't vanish overnight, it lingers in the spaces we forget to clean.

The moon knows my secrets now,

How I trace your name on fogged-up glass.

How I whisper "I miss you" at 2 AM,

And pretend the wind carries it to you.

How I rewrite old conversations,

Searching for a way to make you stay.

But the truth is,

You left long before you walked away.

• 8 •

You didn't just leave, you unraveled everything I believed in.

They told me time would heal,
But time just taught me to pretend.
To laugh at the right moments,
To cry when no one's looking.
To say, "I'm fine" with steady lips,
While my heart trembles beneath.
Time did not heal me,
It just taught me how to hide.

I wish I could unlearn your touch,
Unfeel the warmth of your hands.
Your love still lingers like perfume,
Fading, but never truly gone.
I scrub my skin,
But your fingerprints remain.
How do you forget a love,
That has carved itself into your bones?

I hear your voice in the rain,

In the wind against my window.

Every drop reminds me of you,

And I stand there, letting it drown me.

The storms inside me rage louder,

Than the thunder in the sky.

You were once my shelter,

Now you're the reason I seek cover.

You were my calm, and now I am drowning in the storm you left behind.

I don't hate you,

I don't even blame you.

I just wish you had stayed,

Long enough to see the way you broke me.

To see the pieces left behind,

Scattered like fallen stars.

You wished for the universe,

But I was only the sky.

The hardest part isn't losing you.

It's knowing you're out there,

Loving someone else,

Like I was just a place you passed through.

Like a book you put down halfway,

Never caring for the ending.

I was a story unfinished,

While you turned the page without me.

I keep telling my heart,
That this is the last poem about you.
But it keeps bleeding ink,
And you keep living in my words.
Every syllable tastes like goodbye,
Yet I still write your name in every line.
You left, but you're still here
Between every space and pause.

• 16 •

I keep writing you out of my heart, but somehow, you find your way back into words.

I reach for my phone at midnight,
Still half-expecting a message.
Still hoping you left a "goodnight"
Between the spaces of our silence.
My fingers type and erase,
A hundred unsent texts.
But what's the point of words,
When they never kept you here?

The worst kind of love is the one that teaches you how to miss someone who never looks back.

• 19 •

The mirror shows a girl I don't know,
Her eyes darker, her shoulders heavier.
She used to shine like morning light,
Now she is just another shadow.
Grief has made a home inside her,
And she is too tired to ask it to leave.
She wonders if love was worth it,
If she will ever feel whole again.

I don't know what hurts more, losing you or losing myself trying to keep you.

Some nights, I pretend you never left.
I let my heart rewrite the ending.
One where you stay, where we stay,
Where love doesn't turn into a wound.
Where your hands don't tremble,
When they reach for mine.
Where forever isn't just a word,
But a promise we keep.

• 22 •

I can write the ending a thousand times, but you will still be gone.

• 23 •

Your name still sits on the tip of my tongue,

Like an unfinished sentence.

Like a song that ends too soon,

Like a prayer that was never answered.

I hold onto syllables that burn,

Letters that ache to be spoken.

But some words are better left unsaid,

And some names are meant to fade.

If I could meet the girl I was before you,
I would tell her to run.
To love herself more than your promises,
To never mistake silence for safety.
I would tell her not to stay,
Not to break herself for love.
Because love that asks for sacrifice,
Was never love to begin with.

• 25 •

I deleted your pictures,

Erased your messages.

But how do I forget a love,

That still breathes beneath my skin?

I ripped the pages where we existed,

But the ink has already stained.

I let go of everything I could,

Yet you still remain.

You are gone, but I still wear the ghost of your love on my skin.

Love should not feel like drowning,
It should not leave bruises on the soul.
So why does my heart still whisper your name,
Like an apology I never got?
Why do my hands still tremble,
When someone else reaches for me?
Love should not feel like a wound,
Yet I am still bleeding.

I hope she loves you in ways I couldn't,
And I hope you love her in ways you never loved me.
Because if I suffered for anything,
Let it at least be for your change.
Let my tears have meant something,
Let my heartbreak not be in vain.
I could not make you stay,
But I hope she makes you whole.

They say heartbreak makes you stronger,
But I never asked to be this strong.
I would have chosen love over lessons,
If love had ever chosen me.
I did not want to be a warrior,
I only wanted to be held.
But love made me a battlefield,
And I am still learning how to heal.

One day, I will stop writing about you.
One day, you will be nothing but a memory.
But today is not that day,
And my heart is not yet ready.
Today, I still search for you in strangers,
Still hope for a name I will never hear.
But tomorrow, maybe tomorrow,
I will learn to love myself more than you.

• 31 •

Some stories aren't written to be forgotten, they're felt in silence until they set you free. I still bleed in the spaces you left behind, still trace your name in every almost. But maybe, just maybe, tomorrow I'll choose my own name over yours.

2. The Echoes

Your voice no longer startles me,
But it still lingers in the air.
Like a song I once loved,
Now playing on a broken record.
The echoes don't hurt as much,
But they still remind me of you.
Some wounds stop bleeding,
But they never truly heal,
Only fade into whispers of the past.

Some wounds stop bleeding, but they never forget how to ache.

I walked past our old café today,
And for the first time, I didn't stop.
I didn't search for your reflection,
In the window where we once sat.
The coffee still smells the same,
But it no longer smells like you.
Some memories grow quieter,
But they never fade away,
Just settle like dust in forgotten corners.

I keep running into your ghost,
In places I thought were mine.
You haunt the silence between songs,
And the spaces between my steps.
I don't turn around anymore,
I know you won't be there.
But the past still whispers,
Even when I beg it to stay quiet,
Even when I pretend it no longer exists.

You don't have to turn around to know that past is still watching.

I dreamt of you last night,

But this time, you were leaving.

For once, I wasn't chasing you,

I just stood there, watching.

You didn't look back,

And neither did I.

Maybe my heart is learning,

That not all love is meant to return,

And not all losses are meant to be mourned.

I found an old letter you wrote,
Buried beneath forgotten things.
Your words were soft,
Like the lies you used to tell.
I folded the paper carefully,
Like closing a chapter for good.
Not every love deserves closure,
Some endings write themselves,
And some goodbyes don't need words.

• 39 •

Some goodbyes don't need words, just the strength to walk away.

I don't flinch at your favorite song anymore,
Nor ache at the thought of your smile.
Your ghost still lingers in quiet corners,
But it no longer haunts, it hums and fades.
The nights are softer now,
Less heavy with the weight of what was.
You're not forgotten, just no longer needed.
Love left quietly, like a sigh in sleep.
And I let it go without holding on.

I don't check if you're online anymore,
I don't wonder who you talk to at night.
My heart no longer waits,
For a message that will never come.
I am learning to live without you,
To fill the spaces you left behind.
Some absences remain,
But they no longer ache,
They just exist, quiet and weightless.

The sunrise doesn't ache the way it used to,

When mornings meant your sleepy voice and soft hellos.

Now, the light spills in without echo,

Just silence and peace, no longing.

I sip my coffee without replaying our words,

No pause between breaths, no hidden ache.

Healing is letting stillness settle where noise once lived,

It's waking up without the need to rewind,

And learning to greet the day alone with grace.

But tonight, your name still lingers,

Like smoke in a room I can't escape.

I smile for the world, but inside,

I still flinch at memories dressed as dreams.

Your ghost walks quietly beside me,

Not cruel, just familiar.

And though I ache to forget,

I hold on a little longer.

Not to you, but to who I was when I loved you.

I used to ask myself why,
Why love turned into heartbreak.
Why forever lasted only moments,
Why promises dissolved like mist.
But some questions have no answers,
And some wounds need no reasons.
Sometimes, we just have to accept,
That love is not always meant to last,
And that's not our fault.

Some love stories don't need answers, only endings.

I don't hate you, hate takes too much space,

But I no longer crave your voice or face.

No need for closure, no final word,

The silence now is what I preferred.

Your chapter's done, I've marked the end,

No longer lover, not even friend.

This pen is mine, the script is new,

Each line I write drifts far from you.

No glancing back, just passing through.

I gave myself the closure you never had the courage to offer.

The love I gave was pure and true,
A storm, a flame, a sky of blue.
You held it lightly, let it fall,
As if it never meant at all.
But I won't dim the light I gave,
Or mourn the heart I couldn't save.
For love that's real will never fade,
Even when it's not repaid.
It blooms in silence, unafraid.

I ran into an old friend today,
And they asked about you.
For a moment, I hesitated,
Not sure how to reply.
Then I smiled and simply said,
"He was someone I used to know."
And in that moment,
I realized, I had already moved on,
And you were just a passing thought.

There was a time your love was all I knew,
Like air I breathed, like morning dew.
I thought I'd break if you were gone,
A song unfinished, a fading dawn.
But here I stand, no hand to hold,
A little bruised, but brave and bold.
Love didn't save me from the fall
I rose alone, I faced it all.
Turns out, I was enough after all.

I thought love meant to always fight,
To hold on tight through every night.
But now I see, with clearer eyes,
Love sometimes lives in goodbyes.
It's walking out though fingers shake,
It's choosing peace for your own sake.
Love's not a chain you wear alone,
Nor shattered dreams you build a home.
I won't call ruins my own throne.

Love is also knowing when to stop holding on.

I found peace in the spaces,
Where your absence once lived.
I filled them with laughter,
With the warmth of my own light.
The cracks you left in me,
Have turned into something beautiful.
I thought you were my happy ending,
But I am learning, I am my own,
And I am finally enough.

I've learned to sway where no arms hold,
To smile in silence, fierce and bold.
Joy now blooms in hands once bare,
Not in a gaze or fleeting stare.
Love, I thought, was being claimed,
But now I know, it can't be named.
It lives in breaths I take alone,
In peace that feels like coming home,
And that, I swear, is love full grown.

You were the verse I whispered through tears,
A rhythm that echoed for too many years.
Now you rest in the margins, faint and small,
No longer the reason I rise or fall.
The silence between us speaks more than words,
A song once played, now barely heard.
I turn the page and no backward glance,
This story is mine, not born of chance.
And in these lines, I find my stance.

You were once my poem, now you're just a footnote.

I used to fear letting go,
Thinking love meant holding on.
But I see it now, so clearly
Love also means setting yourself free.
Not every story needs a sequel,
Not every heartache needs a return.
Some loves are meant to end,
So better things can begin,
And I am ready for my beginning.

Not every love story needs a sequel, some are just meant to end. I held on longer than I should've… not because I didn't know how to let go, but because I thought love meant never giving up. Turns out, real love sometimes means walking away with grace, with peace, and with a heart that finally chooses itself. This isn't the end I feared… it's the beginning I deserve.

3. The Rebirth

I opened my eyes, and you weren't the ache anymore,
No whispers of "us" behind the bedroom door.
The mirror holds me with a kinder gaze,
Not lost in the ruins of yesterday's haze.
My breath feels mine, not borrowed in pain,
I dance in the drizzle, not drowned in rain.
No longer stitched to the ghost of your name,
I write new lines, not haunted by shame.
This calm, this fire was never for you,
It's the love I was aching to give me, too.

Healing begins the moment you stop waiting for someone to notice you're broken.

The hands I once held so tightly,
Are no longer the ones I reach for.
I have found comfort in my own grip,
Strength in standing on my own.
Love was never meant to be a cage,
And I was never meant to beg for it.
So I let go, not in sadness,
But with a quiet kind of joy.
Because love should feel like home,
And I am finally home within myself.

I don't trace your voice in the winds at night,
Nor chase your shadow in the morning light.
You were once the prayer behind my tears,
Now just a ghost time slowly clears.
The silence we left no longer screams,
It hums like echoes from old dreams.
You carved your name across my skin,
But healing taught me strength within.
I breathe you out with every sigh-
No longer yours, and I know why.

There is laughter in my voice again,
Not the kind that hides the pain.
It is full, unburdened, real,
Born from the joy I found within.
I do not measure my worth,
By the love you did not give me.
I do not seek validation,
From hands that once let me go.
I am more than the love I lost,
I am the love I choose to give myself.

Losing them was painful. Finding myself was powerful.

I don't bleed your name into verses now,
Not because the wounds have faded somehow,
But because my soul writes softer things,
Like dawns that rise without old strings.
You were once every line I knew,
But love, I've found poems beyond you.
I won't rewrite pain for it to stay,
I choose the light that finds its way.
I didn't lose you, I let me grow.
And that's the most loving way to go.

Some stories aren't unfinished, they just end where they were meant to.

Somewhere along the way,
I stopped waiting for closure.
I realized I did not need it,
To move forward, to be whole.
The past does not deserve,
The power to shape my future.
I give that power to myself,
To build, to grow, to love again.
And when I look ahead,
I see nothing but endless light.

Closure isn't found in answers, it's found in choosing yourself.

I used to fear that love would fade,
That giving too much meant being betrayed.
But hearts aren't meant to lock and hide,
They're made to open, swell with pride.
Some people leave, some promises bend,
But love itself is not the end.
It teaches more than it can take,
It heals the soul each time it breaks.
So here I stand, with arms grown wide
Not empty now, but fortified.

I don't chase the reasons anymore,
Why you closed that open door.
Not every wound needs a name,
To let go without holding blame.
Tears taught me what silence knew,
That healing comes in quiet hues.
No echo now of your goodbye,
Just softer air beneath the sky.
Today, I free what weighed me sore
And take a step, needing you no more.

I saw the sunset today,
And I did not wish for you beside me.
It was beautiful, it was mine,
And I let myself enjoy it alone.
Happiness is no longer something,
I associate with your presence.
It is a song I have learned to sing,
Without needing your harmony.
And for the first time,
It feels like enough.

Some sunsets are best enjoyed alone; with no longing, just peace.

I used to think love meant staying through time,
That forever was proof, and endings a crime.
But now I see truth in the fleeting embrace,
In the smiles that vanish, yet still leave a trace.
You didn't stay, but you still taught me grace,
And in that brief spark, I found my own place.
No bitterness lingers, no anger remains,
Just echoes of laughter and sweet growing pains.
We were real, even if we broke apart,
And I carry that love, not as ache but as art.

The mirror holds more than my face,

It whispers tales I had to chase.

Through silent nights and shattered cries,

I learned to rise from my own lies.

I'm not the girl I used to be,

But strength now walks inside of me.

Love isn't found in flawless skin,

But in the wars I've fought within.

This life is mine, raw, real, and true,

A story inked in shades I drew.

• 75 •

Healing isn't about becoming whole again, it's about embracing who you are now.

My hands don't tremble when your face appears,
Nor do my nights drown in silent tears.
You were a song that softly played,
But not the reason my soul stayed.
I don't resent what slipped away,
It shaped the woman I am today.
Love didn't vanish, it just grew
Not around you, but deep and true.
I found its flame in my own core,
Burning brighter than ever before.

Some chapters don't need closure, just the courage to turn the page.

I once begged the universe,

To bring you back to me.

Now I thank the stars,

For leading me somewhere new.

The love I gave you,

Was never meant to be wasted.

It was meant to teach me,

That I was worthy all along.

And now I walk forward,

Carrying only the love I have for myself.

I won't mistake chaos for care again,
Nor call the storms inside me love.
It took losing myself to understand,
Real love won't make you prove you're enough.
It won't silence dreams or dim your light,
Or leave your heart bruised every night.
Next time it knocks, I'll guard the key,
And wait for arms that set me free.
Not love that burns just to be known,
But one that feels like coming home.

Real love doesn't test your strength, it reminds you that you never had to prove.

I don't see you in the morning light,
Nor in the stars that grace the night.
Your name no longer haunts my sigh,
It's just a breeze that passes by.
Where pain once bloomed, I've sown my grace,
Built softer dreams in your old place.
You weren't the storm that broke me down-
Just fleeting thunder, lost in sound.
I walk a road that's calm and wide,
With nothing of you left inside.

• 82 •

I don't look for you in the past anymore, I look for myself in my future.

• 83 •

I do not fear the night, though it once made me cry,
The moon watched my silence, as stars lit my sky.
I do not flinch at touch, though I once broke apart,
For love didn't shatter me-just the hands, not the heart.
I won't call love cruel, though it once made me ache,
It's the storms, not the sea, that caused the quake.
So when love knocks again under soft silver light,
I won't hide behind shadows or shut out the night.
I'll whisper to the stars, "Let this be enough,"
And wrap my arms around the warmth of love.

• 84 •

Love didn't break me, it only revealed the parts of me that needed healing.

Not every love is built to stay,

Some just pass through like skies of grey.

You were my rainbow after rain,

A burst of light, then gone again.

We danced beneath the weeping shroud,

A fleeting kiss beneath the cloud.

It wasn't false, it wasn't fake,

But some storms leave for healing's sake.

I loved, I lost, but now I see;

True love lets go and sets you free.

• 86 •

Not all love stays, but every love changes us in the ways we never see coming.

I found love again, not in his name,
But in quiet mornings that feel the same.
In coffee sips and messy hair,
In showing up when no one's there.
I healed in truths I used to fear,
In soft-spoken "no's" and wiped-off tears.
Love's not just held in someone's eyes,
It blooms in lows, it soars, it tries.
Now I walk with peace, not just pride,
Whole, unshaken, with me by my side.

The best love story I ever wrote was the one where I chose myself.

This isn't just pain that fades with time,
It's a lesson dressed in quiet rhyme.
She broke, not loud but piece by piece,
Till numbness gave her soul release.
Not in fairytales did she reside,
But in nights where she just cried.
Love didn't kill her, it revealed the scar,
A mirror showing who she really are.
She learned self-worth without applause,
And lives, now whole, without a cause.

I don't check my phone like I used to at night,
Your silence no longer steals sleep from my light.
I've stopped making space where you used to stay,
And filled it with peace that won't drift away.
No longer the girl who begged to be seen,
I've stitched up the wounds where your love had been.
I'm not waiting now for a hand to appear,
The mirror reflects someone strong, someone clear.
Not healed by your absence, nor broken by pain.
But shaped by the storm, and dancing in rain.

There was a time I counted your silence louder than my heartbeat.Now, I rest without waiting, bloom without needing. The girl who once searched for herself in your eyes,Found her whole reflection, within.

4. The Becoming

I no longer wait beneath your sky,
For borrowed stars to teach me why.
The moon once wept with me at night,
Now she glows with my inner light.
I stitched my heart with silver beams,
And filled the cracks with quiet dreams.
No longer dim for someone's spark,
I shine alone within the dark.
This love I found is calm and wide
Like moonlit waves, it holds my tide.
And in its glow, I stand with pride.

The spaces you left empty became the places I grew the most.

I once believed in letters sealed with grace,
That love meant chasing a vanishing face.
I waited like in black-and-white screens,
For a love as pure as vintage scenes.
But fairy tales wore masks too well,
And I mistook a ghost for a wishing well.
You weren't my half, just a fleeting part,
Not the timeless match I gave my heart.
Now I dance to vinyl's gentle spin,
Finding romance quietly, from within
Not in your arms, but in my skin.

• 95 •

I was never missing a piece, you were just never meant to fit.

I have learned to forgive myself,

For the love I gave too freely.

For the hands I held too tightly,

Even when they wanted to let go.

I used to think love was about holding on,

But love is also about release.

And I release you, fully, finally,

Not in bitterness, but in grace.

Not because I did not love you,

But because I love myself more.

Enough to walk away,

Enough to move forward.

You weren't my forever, but you were my song,

The kind that lingers, though the notes feel wrong.

Like ink-stained letters I never could send,

You were a chapter, not the end.

I don't regret the slow-danced nights,

The stolen glances, the whispered fights.

But I lost myself in chasing dreams,

Wove you in threads of hopeless seams.

Now I write in softer ink, just me

No longer trapped in memory.

My heart beats slow, but finally free.

You were the rain I stood in too long, hoping a rainbow would make it worth it.

I once believed in love that waits by the gate,
Letters in drawers and promises of fate.
You were my sepia-toned, slow-dancing song,
But even vintage hearts can get love wrong.
Now your name is just a whispered rain,
Not thunder, not fire, not aching pain.
The past still lingers, but it doesn't burn;
It taught me how deeply souls can yearn.
You weren't my forever, just a prose divine,
A page I turned to finally find mine.
Old love faded, but I kept the shine.

Healing isn't erasing the past, it's learning to live beyond it.

I no longer trace you in whispered air,

Nor ache for words you wouldn't dare.

The love I begged for in silent cries,

Now lives in calm beneath my skies.

I've stitched the silence you left behind,

Into verses only my soul can find.

No prince, no promise, no waiting door;

I am the warmth I once longed for.

If love arrives, it won't define me,

Just walk beside the light inside me.

For I was always enough quietly, completely.

Somewhere between the storms and the blue,
I grew wings where I once broke in two.
No longer a bird trapped in your sky,
I found the courage to learn how to fly.
I don't perch where love feels cold,
Or nest in hands that couldn't hold.
I soar beyond the reach of pain,
Above the clouds, beyond the rain.
I need no wind to lift my flight,
My own truth keeps me in light.
I am my sky, wide, wild, and bright.

Like a sunflower in a forgotten field, she grew anyway rooted in pain, but reaching for hope.

I don't sketch your name on café glass,

Not since the lattes stopped tasting like our past.

The playlist we loved still softly plays,

But it doesn't pause me like those days.

Your laugh once danced through corner seats,

Now silence hums in rhythmic beats.

I sip alone where we once spoke,

Where promises hung like rising smoke.

Our song now ends mid melody,

No encore, no lost remedy.

Just me, and a brew, writing new symphony.

There is lot to say, but I will keep it this way.

Was it love if I had to wait in doubt?
Did roses bloom where silence grew loud?
Can a heart be held through half-spoken words,
Or letters unread, like caged-up birds?
Did you ever mean the songs you played,
Or were they just echoes that slowly fade?
Would real love leave with doors half-shut,
Like vintage films paused in the final cut?
Is love not handwritten notes and eyes that stay
Not games that pull your heart away?
So why should I stay where love forgets to pray?

In love neither the violins will play, nor the wind will stop; it will a calm breeze where your will skip a beat to appreciate it. There won't be any doubts.

This is not the story of heartbreak,
It is the story of rising from it.
Of a girl who gave love freely,
And learned to give it to herself first.
Love did not abandon me,
It simply changed its shape.
And now, it fills the spaces you left,
Not with longing, but with light.
I do not fear love anymore,
Nor do I mourn what was lost.
Because love is not behind me,
It is all around, within, ahead.

She once poured love like rain on barren lands, hoping something would bloom. But when the storms came, she found shelter in her own heart. This isn't a tale of a girl broken; it's of a girl becoming. Of learning that love doesn't disappear, it transforms. And now, where emptiness used to echo, there's warmth, grace, and light. She doesn't chase love anymore; she is it.

5. The After

I swore the moon would never move me again,
Not after nights it watched me break in vain.
The stars once mocked my tear-stained face,
Flickering truths I refused to embrace.
But now you come with eyes like skies,
And something in me softly sighs.
The warmth returns, both sweet and strange,
Yet fear walks close, afraid of change.
What if your light is just a phase;
A passing glow that slowly decays?
Do I reach, or let the moment fade?
Beneath the stars, my choice is made.

*Just when I had folded away the letters and sealed the diary shut,
love arrived with ink-stained hands and vintage soul.*

Your eyes don't chase, they simply stay,
Like dawn unfolding at the edge of day.
You don't ask me to forget the pain,
Or promise sun without the rain.
You see the cracks and don't look away,
You hold the silence like it's okay.
I've built my walls from years gone wrong,
But something about you feels like a song.
Not loud, not wild, just soft and true;
A rhythm I might one day dance to.
So here I stand, not ready to fall,
But thinking... maybe I could risk it all.

My scars still speaks in silence, but your patience listens the unsaid.

I tell myself to stay ashore,

To fear the pull I've felt before.

But love, like tides, ignores my plea,

It rushes in—wild, like the sea.

No warning buoys, no anchored line,

Just waves that whisper, "You'll be fine."

I brace myself, but still I sway,

Drawn deeper with each breath, each day.

Is this a storm, or something rare?

A drift toward truth, or just thin air?

I swore I'd never swim that far again;

But here I float, forgetting when.

Sometimes love isn't found in the waves we chase, but in the calm after we stop running from the sea.

I search for red flags in your words,

For signs that history will repeat.

I question your kindness,

As if love must come with conditions.

I wonder if this is too soon,

If I am running towards another storm.

But your presence does not suffocate,

It does not feel like borrowed time.

You do not make me smaller,

Or ask me to forget my past.

You simply stand there,

And let me find my way to you.

What if love is like the evening tea I pour;
Warm, uncertain, steeped in something more?
The steam curls like questions in the air,
Fragile hopes laced with silent prayer.
Its scent reminds me of past goodbyes,
Yet comforts me as the old ache dies.
I sip, though I know it may someday burn,
Still, there are lessons in each return.
I've stitched my soul from shattered glass,
So fear, like sugar, will surely pass.
Love may not stay, but I'll still choose
The cup, the scent, and all I could lose.

The risk isn't in falling, it's in never letting myself try again.

You do not complete me, nor do I need the fix,

For in my own soul, I've found what's worth the risk.

I'm not a puzzle, broken or in search of cure,

I'm whole, and with you, that feels pure.

I come not as a dreamer lost in some tale,

But as a woman whose own strength will never fail.

You don't promise me the moon, nor the stars above,

Just a place beside you, with your simple love.

No flawless story, no end that's written clear,

Just two souls that know sorrow, but choose to stay near.

With hearts that have learned, and scars that remain,

We dare to love again, through the joy and the pain.

What if I let myself love you,

Not with desperation, but with peace?

Not with the fear of losing,

But with the joy of what is now?

What if love is not about forever,

But about the moments we choose?

The late night laughter,

The silent understanding,

The way your hand finds mine,

Without hesitation, without demand,

As if love could be simple, If only I let it be.

Maybe love is showing up, choosing and staying.

There's a part of me that still hides at night,
Afraid love's spark might burn too bright.
But under stars that never rush,
My fears grow quiet, my thoughts hush.
Maybe love is not a storm to flee,
But constellations guiding me.
A hand that holds, not pulls apart,
A calm eclipse upon my heart.
I don't know where this path may go,
If it'll stay or softly snow.
But in the glow of starlit doubt,
I close my eyes... and let hope out.

Fear in me still lingers, but hope is starting to whisper louder.

I brace for winds that never blow,
Like autumn leaves too scared to go.
Love, for me, was always cold,
A fleeting warmth I couldn't hold.
But you arrive like early fall,
Not loud, just calm, not rushed at all.
You don't demand what I can't give,
You show me love in how you live.
Like trees that shed and still stand tall,
You teach me I won't lose it all.
Maybe love's not fire or flight
But the golden hush before the night.

• 125 •

Love doesn't have to be loud to be real; sometimes, it's the quiet that stays.

I wonder if you see my fears,
If you notice the way I hesitate.
I want to trust in what we are,
But old wounds whisper warnings.
What if I let myself love you,
Only to watch you walk away?
But then you reach for my hand,
Not to pull me, not to lead
Just to remind me that you're here.
And maybe, just maybe,
That is all I need,
For now.

You don't pull me forward, you don't push me back; you just remind me you are here.

I see it in the way old hands still touch,
Wrinkled, but holding on just as much.
They do not speak in grand, loud tones,
But love in silences, in softened bones.
Some days I feel that kind of grace—
Where love is slow, not some frantic chase.
I sit beside you and feel the years,
Not in age, but in quiet fears.
What if I'm not broken, just learning to stay?
To choose love in a gentler way.
No forever carved in stone or sky,
Just you and me, giving it one more try.

I swore the moon would never move me again,
Not after nights it watched me break in vain.
The stars once mocked my tear-stained face,
Flickering truths I refused to embrace.
But now you come with eyes like skies,
And something in me softly sighs.
The warmth returns, both sweet and strange,
Yet fear walks close, afraid of change.
What if your light is just a phase;
A passing glow that slowly decays?
Do I reach, or let the moment fade?
Beneath the stars, my choice is made.

• 130 •

Just when I had folded away the letters and sealed the diary shut,
love arrived with ink-stained hands and vintage soul.

Your eyes don't chase, they simply stay,
Like dawn unfolding at the edge of day.
You don't ask me to forget the pain,
Or promise sun without the rain.
You see the cracks and don't look away,
You hold the silence like it's okay.
I've built my walls from years gone wrong,
But something about you feels like a song.
Not loud, not wild, just soft and true;
A rhythm I might one day dance to.
So here I stand, not ready to fall,
But thinking... maybe I could risk it all.

My scars still speaks in silence, but your patience listens the unsaid.

I tell myself to stay ashore,

To fear the pull I've felt before.

But love, like tides, ignores my plea,

It rushes in—wild, like the sea.

No warning buoys, no anchored line,

Just waves that whisper, "You'll be fine."

I brace myself, but still I sway,

Drawn deeper with each breath, each day.

Is this a storm, or something rare?

A drift toward truth, or just thin air?

I swore I'd never swim that far again;

But here I float, forgetting when.

• 134 •

Sometimes love isn't found in the waves we chase, but in the calm after we stop running from the sea.

I search for red flags in your words,

For signs that history will repeat.

I question your kindness,

As if love must come with conditions.

I wonder if this is too soon,

If I am running towards another storm.

But your presence does not suffocate,

It does not feel like borrowed time.

You do not make me smaller,

Or ask me to forget my past.

You simply stand there,

And let me find my way to you.

What if love is like the evening tea I pour;
Warm, uncertain, steeped in something more?
The steam curls like questions in the air,
Fragile hopes laced with silent prayer.
Its scent reminds me of past goodbyes,
Yet comforts me as the old ache dies.
I sip, though I know it may someday burn,
Still, there are lessons in each return.
I've stitched my soul from shattered glass,
So fear, like sugar, will surely pass.
Love may not stay, but I'll still choose
The cup, the scent, and all I could lose.

The risk isn't in falling, it's in never letting myself try again.

You do not complete me, nor do I need the fix,

For in my own soul, I've found what's worth the risk.

I'm not a puzzle, broken or in search of cure,

I'm whole, and with you, that feels pure.

I come not as a dreamer lost in some tale,

But as a woman whose own strength will never fail.

You don't promise me the moon, nor the stars above,

Just a place beside you, with your simple love.

No flawless story, no end that's written clear,

Just two souls that know sorrow, but choose to stay near.

With hearts that have learned, and scars that remain,

We dare to love again, through the joy and the pain.

What if I let myself love you,
Not with desperation, but with peace?
Not with the fear of losing,
But with the joy of what is now?
What if love is not about forever,
But about the moments we choose?
The late night laughter,
The silent understanding,
The way your hand finds mine,
Without hesitation, without demand,
As if love could be simple, If only I let it be.

Maybe love is showing up, choosing and staying.

There's a part of me that still hides at night,

Afraid love's spark might burn too bright.

But under stars that never rush,

My fears grow quiet, my thoughts hush.

Maybe love is not a storm to flee,

But constellations guiding me.

A hand that holds, not pulls apart,

A calm eclipse upon my heart.

I don't know where this path may go,

If it'll stay or softly snow.

But in the glow of starlit doubt,

I close my eyes... and let hope out.

• 142 •

Fear in me still lingers, but hope is starting to whisper louder.

I brace for winds that never blow,

Like autumn leaves too scared to go.

Love, for me, was always cold,

A fleeting warmth I couldn't hold.

But you arrive like early fall,

Not loud, just calm, not rushed at all.

You don't demand what I can't give,

You show me love in how you live.

Like trees that shed and still stand tall,

You teach me I won't lose it all.

Maybe love's not fire or flight

But the golden hush before the night.

Love doesn't have to be loud to be real; sometimes, it's the quiet that stays.

I wonder if you see my fears,

If you notice the way I hesitate.

I want to trust in what we are,

But old wounds whisper warnings.

What if I let myself love you,

Only to watch you walk away?

But then you reach for my hand,

Not to pull me, not to lead

Just to remind me that you're here.

And maybe, just maybe,

That is all I need,

For now.

You don't pull me forward, you don't push me back; you just remind me you are here.

I see it in the way old hands still touch,

Wrinkled, but holding on just as much.

They do not speak in grand, loud tones,

But love in silences, in softened bones.

Some days I feel that kind of grace—

Where love is slow, not some frantic chase.

I sit beside you and feel the years,

Not in age, but in quiet fears.

What if I'm not broken, just learning to stay?

To choose love in a gentler way.

No forever carved in stone or sky,

Just you and me, giving it one more try.

I kept the teddy you gave that year,
Worn at the seams, but still held near.
A note you wrote, now faint with age,
Tucked in my drawer like a fragile page.
For years, I clung to what we were,
Afraid to feel, afraid to stir.
But then you came not with grand displays,
Just quiet eyes that held my maze.
You didn't ask me to be whole,
You touched the corners of my soul.
You waited where the past still stayed,
And loved me gently, not afraid.

I am not something broken to be fixed, I am something whole, still unfolding.

I don't need a map for where we might go,
Some stories bloom soft, not fast or in show.
You don't need to swear on forever's name,
Just walk beside me, slow and the same.
I've known the ache of love that burned bright,
And vanished like stars before morning light.
But this feels like letters in a faded book,
A glance, a pause, the way you look.
Not fireworks, but a steady flame
No games to play, no hearts to tame.
If love begins here, unsure yet true,
Then let it unfold, like old souls do.

The beauty of love isn't in forever, but in choosing it, moment by moment.

I do not love you yet,
But the thought no longer scares me.
Love does not have to be rushed,
It does not have to be urgent.
It can be slow, like dawn breaking,
Like petals unfolding in the sun.
I do not need to know the ending,
To appreciate the beauty of the beginning.
So I stand here, open and uncertain,
Not demanding answers,
Not fearing the unknown,
But simply letting love grow.

I won't lose myself in loving you,

I've done that once, it broke me in two.

But if you'd like, stay for this tea,

By the café window, just you and me.

The rain taps soft on the glass so clear,

Like all the words we're too scared to hear.

No promises made, no futures drawn,

Just warmth in the moment before it's gone.

Love need not burn to leave a mark,

It can be gentle, steady, and stark.

And if we drift like clouds in rain,

I'll still remember us without pain.

Maybe this time will be different,

Or maybe it will end the same way.

Maybe I will find a love that stays,

Or maybe I will learn another lesson.

I do not know, and that is the beauty of it.

Love is not about certainty,

It is about stepping forward despite the fear.

And if I get hurt again,

I will not break,

I will not shatter.

Because I have already risen once,

And I will rise again,

No matter what comes next.

I see you there, and time stands still,
A moment soft, against my will.
Your eyes don't promise, yet they stay,
Like dawn unsure if it's night or day.
I don't pretend to know what's true,
But something tender pulls me to you.
It's not a fairytale, not a game;
Just two hearts scared, but not the same.
I feel the ache, the silent plea,
Of love that asks, "Can you choose me?"
No answers rise, just stars that shine,
And a trembling hope, "maybe this time".

I once cried beneath the mourning moon,
Swore love had left my life too soon.
But now its glow feels soft, not cold,
A silver hush where dreams unfold.
He's not a promise carved in stone,
But in his eyes, I'm not alone.
No stars aligned, no grand design,
Just quiet moments that feel divine.
I still flinch at echoes of the past,
Yet breathe in hope, however vast.
The moon and I, both bruised but steady
Whisper to the night, "I think I'm ready."

Once, I wrote about heartbreak. Today, I write about hope.

A gentle breeze moves through my hair,
Like whispers from a world that cares.
There's a softness in the air tonight,
A quiet pull toward morning light.
Though my past still flickers in my chest,
My heart now beats with kinder unrest.
I do not chase what used to be,
I walk ahead, wild and free.
The path is misted, unclear, unknown,
But I no longer walk it alone.
The wind hums songs I've yet to hear
And I lean into love, without the fear.

The ink has dried on what we were, A chapter closed, no need to blur. The pages torn, the margins stained, But still, my story has remained. Your name's a line in yesterday, I've learned I'm more than what you say.

The spine is worn, the cover creased, But from that pain, I found release. No longer trapped in scenes we wrote, I breathe between each healing note. A plot untwists, a thread runs free, This book now turns because of me.

I do not fear the words ahead, Though some are soft and some are bled. Each risk I take, each truth I face, Is written with a quiet grace. For even heartbreak has its place, It taught my soul to love its space.

So here I am with trembling pen, Not asking how or even when. I write with wonder, not with ache, A story only I can make. And in the footnotes of my pain, Lives the strength to try again.

This is not my story, this is our story.

The End

And so, this isn't where the story ends only where she stops chasing what was never hers. Where heartbreak becomes memory, and memory becomes the soil for something softer, stronger, and truer.

She no longer waits at closed doors. She no longer writes poems for the ones who left. Now, she writes for herself. For beginnings that don't need permission, for endings that don't require apologies, and for love that finally stays.

This is not the story of what was lost. This is the story of what was found, after all the almosts. After all the ache. After all the silence.

This...is her becoming. This...is "The Poetry of Almost".